CREATING A HUMMINGBIRD GARDEN

D1125561

CREATING A HUMMINGBIRD GARDEN

A Guide to Attracting
and Identifying Hummingbird Visitors

by Marcus Schneck

A Fireside Book
Published by Simon & Schuster Inc.
New York London Toronto Sydney Tokyo Singapore

Fireside
Simon & Schuster Building
Rockefeller Center
1230 Avenue of the Americas
New York, New York 10020
Copyright © 1993 Quarto Publishing Inc.

This book was designed and produced by
Quarto Publishing Inc. The Old Brewery
6 Blundell Street London N7 9BH

SENIOR EDITOR Sally MacEachern
COPY EDITOR Maggi McCormick
SENIOR ART EDITOR Amanda Bakhtiar
DESIGNER Sheila Volpe
ILLUSTRATORS Wayne Ford,
Paul Richardson, Sally Launder

ART DIRECTOR Moira Clinch
EDITORIAL DIRECTOR Sophie Collins
TYPESET BY Diamond Graphics
MANUFACTURED BY Eray Scan,
Singapore
PRINTED BY Leefung Asco Printers Ltd,
China

10 9 8 7 6 5

Library of Congress Cataloging in
Publication Data

Schneck, Marcus.
        Creating a hummingbird garden: a
guide to attracting and identifying
hummingbird visitors/by Marcus Schneck.
            p.   cm.
        "A Fireside book."
        Includes index.
        ISBN 0-671-89245-2 : $8.95
        1. Gardening to attract birds.
2. Hummingbirds. 3. Hummingbirds-
Identification. I. Title.
QL676.5.S325 1993   93-43136
639.9'7899--dc20.   CIP

CONTENTS

HUMMERS LOVE BACKYARDS

There's no doubt about it. Most species of hummingbirds love what many of us have done with backyards. Even without any special planning or forethought, many of the brightly flowering plants that we love to have in abundance serve the tiny, feathered "helicopters" equally well.

Whether those flowers – particularly red and orange ones – appear on our highly manicured ornamental plants, in our flower gardens, or as part of specially designed backyard habitats for hummingbirds and/or other wild creatures, they have become meccas for the nectar-sipping birds. Such places quickly become part of a hummingbird's daily rounds, possibly warranting more than a single visit each day.

Our gardens, intentionally or otherwise, have become part of the forefront in hummingbird conservation. And these tiny birds, like so many wildlife species, need all the help they can find.

We're far removed from those days in the mid-1800s when hundreds of thousands of hummingbirds were killed and exported to Europe for use in specimen collections, ornamentation on ladies' hats and similar applications. But we've come up with even more dangerous threats in the pesticides, herbicides and all the other "cides" that we apply to our properties in the name of green lawns.

If you're thinking about attracting hummingbirds to your backyard, your first step – the kindest, most caring thing you can do – is to cease using all chemicals. Be assured, nearly all those pesticides and herbicides are quite deadly to your little visitors.

▲ *The flowers that fill our gardens have bolstered many hummingbird species in the face of declining natural habitat.*

BACKYARDS AND HUMMINGBIRDS

Please don't come to the wrong conclusion after reading the previous pages of this book. Yes, humans have greatly damaged nearly all populations of hummingbirds. Some appear to have been hunted to extinction before they were even identified and classified. However, more recent developments on our part have been more beneficial to the birds.

In the western regions of North America, where periodic droughts and the accompanying shortfalls in natural, wild plants had for centuries limited the range of some hummingbird species, our backyard habitats, flowering gardens and ornamental plants have provided the boost that these species needed to expand. For example, some pretty definite correlations can be drawn between the expansion of the range occupied by the Anna's hummingbird and the expansion of land occupied by human dwellings and their backyards. Habitat was no longer a limiting factor for the species.

Whether intentionally or purely by coincidence, we've provided the hummingbirds with a smorgasbord, often on sites that previously produced nectar-filled flowers only in those years when weather conditions were just right. Today, with our application of water even during the dry periods, we cause those spots to produce every year, often for longer periods each year. Hummingbirds have been quick to take advantage of this situation.

◀▶ *In the southwestern United States, where the Costa's Hummingbird makes its home, periodic droughts and generally dry conditions naturally limited the range that the species could occupy. However, the flower-packed gardens with unnaturally regular waterings that humans established throughout the region have helped the birds to expand their range.*

THE PERFECT FLOWER

Look to the bill of the hummingbird, and you'll see the shape of the flower best suited to giving up its nectar to the bird. Long, thin and pointed, that bill is designed for reaching down into narrow, tubular openings. However, it is a common misconception that the nectar is sucked through the bill. In reality, the nectar is pumped along the top of the bird's tongue, which extends even further than its bill.

Look to the metabolism of the hummingbird – among the highest of all warm-blooded creatures – and you'll understand that the perfect hummingbird flower produces heavy supplies of nectar. Energy consumption in hummingbirds is so high that they must feed almost constantly during the daylight hours. They must gain as much as they can from every flower they visit.

Look to the hummingbird's method of flight – constantly whirring wings – and you'll know why the birds prefer to feed at flowers growing on the outside of the plant, where they won't strike their wings. Hanging, pendant flowers, like those of the fuchsia, are particularly attractive to the birds.

▶ *Tubular and pendant-like flowers, and the elongated beak and tongue of the hummingbird have evolved over thousands of generations to complement each other perfectly and to facilitate interaction. The bird gets nectar and in turn helps to pollinate the flower.*

RED: THE PERFECT COLOR

In the world of the hummingbird, there's nothing quite as alluring as the color red. The tiny birds will examine flowers of other colors and will take nectar from them, but the red flowers will generally draw them first and strongest. All shades of red, from pink to orange, hold this amazing power, although the more brilliant shades appear to have an edge.

The fragrance of the flowers appears to play a secondary role in attracting the hummingbirds to feed. And, even non-flower surfaces in shades of red – such as laundry dangling from the washline or a discarded bottle cap – have demonstrated strong pulling power over the birds.

This fact has not escaped the attention of the bird supply industry. It is the reason that red plastic has been incorporated into so many different styles of hummingbird feeders. It is the reason that so many hummingbird nectar mixes contain red dye, which should be avoided so as not to introduce chemicals into the birds' systems.

▲ *These red salvia flowers are very attractive to hummingbirds.*

PLANNING THE GARDEN

In developing the land around your home to attract and be useful to any sort of wild creatures, planning the site should always begin with a good look at what already exists there. Maybe you already have hummingbird visitors. What plants are they visiting?

If you already have one of the many beneficial wild, native plants such as cardinal flower or trumpet creeper growing on the site and bringing hummingbirds there, you probably don't want to remove those plants simply because you've decided to take a more proactive approach. The same could also be said for non-native plants. Perhaps the existing plant, or plants, already attracting hummingbirds could become one of the building blocks for your new backyard.

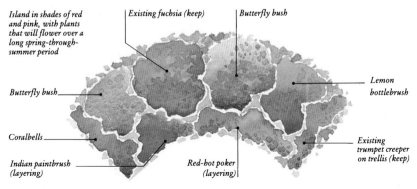

Island in shades of red and pink, with plants that will flower over a long spring-through-summer period

Existing fuchsia (keep)

Butterfly bush

Lemon bottlebrush

Butterfly bush

Coralbells

Indian paintbrush (layering)

Red-hot poker (layering)

Existing trumpet creeper on trellis (keep)

Each existing feature should be considered in this way and judged on its merits. If it stays, sketch it roughly on a scale diagram of the site. After the garden as it now exists has been completely surveyed in this informal manner, you can begin to add new features on the diagram. By doing this all on paper, you will save yourself a great deal of wasted or misdirected effort. When you have a site on paper that satisfies your goals and desires, then you can begin to make the actual changes out there in the backyard.

A common mistake among those new to the concept of backyard wildlife habitats, including habitats for the hummingbirds, is to occupy the entire site with the habitat. They tend to exclude human activities from the site. Don't forget to save some space for yourself.

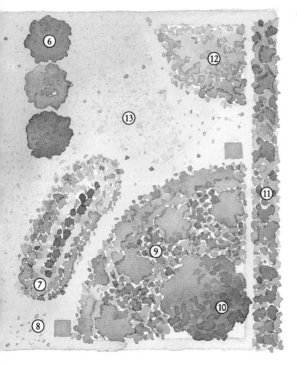

GARDEN PLAN
1 *House*
2 *Deck*
3 *Steps*
4 *Bird bath*
5 *Existing ornamental flower bed*
6 *Existing shrubs*
7 *Island of hummingbird flowers – red-hot poker, petunia, shrimp-plant*
8 *Hummingbird feeder*
9 *Hummingbird flower bed – monkey flower, nasturtium, scarlet begonia, petunia, scarlet runner bean, coral fountain*
10 *Flowering maple*
11 *Trellis with trumpet vine*
12 *Cape honeysuckle*
13 *Open lawn*

LAYERING IN THE GARDEN

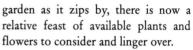

 garden that's been arranged with layering in mind presents a wonderfully diverse front. Rising from the shorter plants in the front through the mid-sized plants to the tallest plants at the back, the layered garden offers the greatest variety of sizes, shapes, textures, hues and colors at any given spot. It's a constant feast for the eyes.

The layered garden has the same impact on the hummingbird. In place of just one or two offerings that the bird might be able to spot in the non-layered garden as it zips by, there is now a relative feast of available plants and flowers to consider and linger over.

And, as the hummingbird moves among the plants, from one layer to the next, the layered garden offers a much more unobstructed view of the bird's activities for the hummingbird watcher. It's impossible never to lose sight of a hummingbird, even during a short period of watching, but the layered garden lessens the "disappearing act" of the swift flier.

◀▲ *Gradually elevated
slopes of flowers present
the most enticing setting
to hummers.*

GARDEN ISLANDS

When we think of layering in the garden, we tend to pigeonhole our vision to only the outline of the property, the edge of the garden. But layering can also be moved into the center of the garden and other non-edge sites.

Island-like designs can be achieved anywhere in the garden if we adopt a more three-dimensional outlook on the site. A crescent-shaped patch of flowering plants, layered to a high-point at the center of the crescent and separated from other flowering areas of the garden by an expanse of open lawn, is not only pleasing to the eye but welcomed by hummingbirds. Other shapes, as simple as a circle or as complicated as a star, fit this plan equally well.

With a series of parallel or otherwise complementary garden islands,

again separated by open lawn, we might create our own miniature versions of the hedgerow maze. The grassy pathways between such garden islands are delightful places to stroll. In addition, the interspersing of islands with lawn provides a multitude of additional feeding places for the hummingbird.

As variations on the island concept, raised beds sided with timbers might be used to form the island boundaries, or the lawn pathways might be replaced with stone or wood chips. The most important factor is that the garden becomes a place where you want to spend time.

◀ *Planting flower beds as "islands" throughout the garden increases the flower-surface area for hummingbird use.*

VINES, SHRUBS, AND TREES

When we think of hummingbirds and the plants that attract and nurture them, we usually envision beds of flowers or rolling meadows of wildflowers. After all, these are the types of environments where we expect to find the tiny birds flitting about.

However, there is no need to stop waist-high when considering a hummingbird garden. There are many fine taller plants that can bring an added dimension to your garden, as well as food sources for the hummingbirds.

For example, the common butterfly bush, a shrub that can grow as tall as 10 feet, could just as easily have been named the hummingbird bush by the first observers. Its profusion of white or lavender flowers provides ample nectar for either group.

The trumpet creeper or trumpet vine provides a wonderful bloom of orange and red flowers from July to September. Hummingbirds, along with a myriad of nectar-seeking insects, are attracted to those flowers as if they were magnets. And the vine takes

easily to the trellis, arbor or similar supports, spanning them with up to 30 feet of length.

And hummingbirds certainly aren't hesitant to fly even higher for their nectar. Trees like the silk oak, which can top 50 feet in height, offer some wonderfully attractive flowers for hummingbirds and an opportunity to add a bit of shade for yourself.

◄ ► *Many species and cultivars of shrubs, such as honeysuckle, and vines, such as the trumpet vine, provide nectar-filled flowers as attractive to hummingbirds as any of the more typical flower bed plants. They can be used to offer flowers at greater heights, increasing the overall garden attraction.*

THE SPRING GARDEN

On some parts of the continent, the first hummingbirds will arrive in early to mid-spring, before many flowers are in bloom. This puzzled observers, scientists and amateurs alike, for many years. What were the birds eating to survive until the flowers appeared?

More recently, the secrets of this puzzling ability have been revealed. The ruby-throated hummingbird, for example, regularly makes its northward flight from Central America across the Gulf of Mexico and throughout the eastern half of North America well in advance of summer's flowers. We now know that the hummingbirds find a substantial portion of their food during the pre-flower period by following yellow-bellied sapsuckers and drinking from the "wells" that the larger birds drill in trees to collect sap. The

hummingbirds take advantage not only of the sap in the wells, but of the insects attracted to it as well. Other early-migrating species have adapted similar survival strategies.

You can bring your hummingbird garden into the mix of these strategies by including plenty of early flowering species of plants, such as red weigela, columbine, lupine and Japanese flowering quince. Also, position your hummingbird feeders and fill them with their sugar-water mixture early in the spring, well before the traditional season for these fixtures.

Any early-season preparations that you make will be amply rewarded by any hummingbirds in your area. Few other gardeners will have gone to such bother, leaving your garden shining like a food-rich magnet in a near-desert of food shortage.

▲ *Early-flowering*
cultivars are essential to
attract hummingbirds into
the garden during the
spring, while awaiting the
greater profusion to come.

SPRING GARDEN

1 *Red-hot poker*
2 *Dwarf nasturtium*
3 *Petunia*
4 *Begonia*
5 *Shrimp plant*
6 *Silk oak*
7 *Rosemary*

8 *Lantana*
9 *Ocotillo*
10 *Monkey flower*
11 *Rosemary grevillea*
12 *Japanese honeysuckle*
13 *Woolly Bluecurls*
14 *Lemon bottlebrush*

SPRING PLANTS

RED-HOT POKER*
Holds its bloom from spring through much of summer in most regions.

DWARF NASTURTIUM
Tropaeolum majus var.
Grows to 1 foot
Annual
Begin indoors and transplant as seedling or sow directly after last frost of spring
Slightly sandy, well-drained soil Sun-loving

PETUNIA
Petunia hybrida
Grows to 1½ feet
Annual
Dead-head
Well-drained, light soil
Sunny location

BEGONIA
Begonia semperflorens
Grows to 1½ feet
Perennial
Generally will not overwinter north of Zone 9
Rich, well-composted soil
Partial shade

SHRIMP PLANT
Beloperone guttata
Grows to 3 feet
Deciduous
Requires regular feeding during the growing season
Well-composted soil
Partial shade

---

*For gardening facts, see pages 50-1.

Lantana

SILK OAK
Grevillea robusta
Grows to 50 feet
Evergreen
Needs extra protection in winter north of Zone 8
Not fussy about soil conditions
Full sun

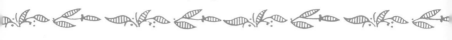

ROSEMARY
Rosmarinus officinalis
Grows to 6½ feet
Evergreen
Needs extra protection in
winter north of Zone 8
Not fussy about soil
conditions
Full sun

LANTANA
Lantana camara
Grows to 10 feet
Evergreen from Zone 8
south; annual to the
north
From Zone 9 south this
plant can self-seed and
become a nuisance
Rich, well-composted
soil
Full sun

OCOTILLO*
Needs excellent drainage.
Avoid overwatering after
it flowers.

MONKEY FLOWER*
Prune after the first
flowering in summer to
encourage a second
bloom period in late
summer or early fall.

ROSEMARY
GREVILLEA
Grevillea rosmarinifolia
Grows to 6 feet
Evergreen
Requires extra winter
protection north of
Zone 9
Not fussy about soil
conditions
Full sun

JAPANESE
HONEYSUCKLE
Lonicera japonica
Grows to 30 feet
Semi-evergreen
Cool, moist soil
Semi-shaded location

WOOLLY
BLUECURLS
Trichostema lanatum
Grows to 5 feet
Evergreen
Well-adapted to various
soil types
Full sun

LEMON
BOTTLEBRUSH*
Very tolerant of full sun,
drought and poor soil
conditions.

NESTING NEEDS

Each species of hummingbird has its own special nest-building preferences.

The ruby-throated hummingbird, for example, builds its nest of downy plant materials, scales from plant buds and bits of leaves, hiding the whole array under an exterior coating of lichens. Strands of spider's web are employed to attach the nest to the upper side of a horizontal limb, generally in hickory, oak, pine or tulip-poplar trees.

By contrast, the calliope hummingbird weaves bark, leaves, moss and plant matter down into its tight little cup of a nest, adding an exterior layer of pine-cone segments. It is often built on top of the same female's nest from the previous year. Coniferous trees seem to be preferred.

Coinciding with the miniature scale of their builders, most hummingbird nests are quite small, usually no more than 1½ inches in exterior diameter.

Horizontal tree limbs, generally with other limbs overhanging and sheltering them, are important to a majority of hummingbird species. However, nests have been discovered on many surfaces, including light fixtures and laundry left on the clothesline for extended periods.

Most species will bring off only one brood of young each year, although the Allen's and rufous species raise two broods, and the Anna's and black-chinned can raise three.

▶ *The nest of most species is a delicate but well-made structure, as small and difficult to spot as its maker.*

FEEDERS

When a steady and ample source of nectar is involved, nearly all hummingbirds are fearless and bold in returning again and again to that source of nectar. This characteristic makes it possible for us to bring the tiny birds quite close to whatever window or other vantage point we want.

But the hummingbirds in your area may take a frustratingly long time to find your feeder initially, unless they are already frequenting your property as a source of natural flower nectar. You can help the discovery process along by using a feeder with as much bright red coloring on it as you can find. Do not, however, add red dye or food coloring to your nectar mix. As mentioned previously, the birds do not need this additional artificial substance in their systems.

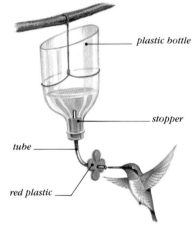

plastic bottle

stopper

tube

red plastic

Place your feeders no farther than 15 feet from the nearest cover, where the birds can quickly escape if threatened, and no closer than 15 feet to any window, where the birds can injure themselves by flying into the glass or screen.

◀▶ *Hummingbird feeders are available in many different sizes and designs. Some, without perches, require the birds to maintain flight while feeding. Others, with perching spots, allow the birds to rest before, during and after they have fed. Both will attract hummingbirds to regular visits, however the latter encourages them to remain still temporarily for better viewing and simpler photography.*

RECIPES

Many different nectar recipes have been developed and championed over the years. Most will attract hummingbirds, but the most beneficial to the birds will be a mix of not more than one part sugar to four parts water. Non-tapwater or tapwater that has been allowed to outgas most of the chlorine and other chemicals that humans add to their drinking supply is preferred, as hummingbirds have been observed to avoid heavily chlorinated waters. Stir the sugar into the water and bring the mixture to a boil.

As important as the nectar mixture you settle upon is regular cleaning of the feeder. Sugar-water mixtures are breeding grounds for organisms that can sicken and kill the hummingbirds . Every day should be your schedule in hot weather, while every three or four days will be fine in cooler weather.

WARNING

- You can make a nectar mixture from any type of sugar. However, do not use honey, fruit sweeteners, or any other common sweetener.
- Do not use ammonia-based products to clean the feeder. It is best to dissolve an effervescent tablet of dental cleanser in warm water. Soak the feeder in it overnight, swab out with a bristle brush and rinse well with fresh water. You can also use soap, providing you rinse well afterward.

▶ *Red dye, as used in this homemade nectar, is not necessary to attract hummingbirds to feeders and may harm them.*

THE SUMMER GARDEN

lthough the first humming-birds will appear in the garden in the springtime, summer is really the season of the hummingbird for most of North America. To a garden that is in its heaviest and most colorful bloom of the year, the birds add their darting, shimmering forms.

Migration is behind this annual timing of the hummingbirds as they move between wintering and breeding grounds. The ruby-throated humming-bird, which is the only species that nests east of the Mississippi River, makes its migratory flight each spring and fall across the Gulf of Mexico, between North America and Central America. The rufous hummingbird, which nests as far north as Alaska, makes its migra-tory way along the Rockies and Cas-cades, between northwestern North America and Central America.

Regardless of the reasons for this phenomenon, summer is the most magical of times in the hummingbird garden. The birds have staked out their territories, through which they travel regular routes several times each day. Soon the younger birds of the year will begin to appear with the adults, snatching up insects and hovering over the nectar flowers.

◀ *What hummingbird could pass through this garden without stopping to take some nectar from such a large and diverse selection? Summer is the height of the flowering season for gardens throughout the country, and therefore the height of the hummingbird season as well.*

SUMMER GARDEN

1 *Eucalyptus*
2 *Ocotillo*
3 *Lantana*
4 *Red-hot poker*
5 *Nicotiana*
6 *Lemon bottlebrush*
7 *Dwarf nasturtium*
8 *Shrimp plant*
9 *Monkey flower*

10 *Scarlet runner bean*
11 *Begonia*
12 *Petunia*
13 *Rosemary*
14 *Abutilon*
15 *Japanese honeysuckle*
16 *Fuchsia*
17 *Orange tree*

SUMMER PLANTS

Eucalyptus

EUCALYPTUS
Eucalyptus spp.
Varying heights
Evergreen
Needs extra winter
protection north of
Zone 8
Well-drained soil
Full sun

OCOTILLO*
The scarlet flowers that
began in spring are now
in full bloom.

LANTANA†
The flowering season
continues nearly year-
round in southern zones,
through summer in
northern zones.

RED-HOT POKER*
The flowering season is
long, running from early
spring well into summer.

NICOTIANA
*Nicotiana alata
grandiflora*
Grows to 3 feet
Annual
Best started from
nursery-grown stock
transplanted after danger
of frost has passed
Well-composted, well-
drained soil
Full sun

**LEMON
BOTTLEBRUSH***
The flowering season is
nearly year-round in
southern zones, and will
run through the summer
in northern zones.

**DWARF
NASTURTIUM†**
The flowers will remain
throughout the summer.

SHRIMP PLANT†
Except in the southern
zones, the flowers will
begin to disappear by late
summer

MONKEY FLOWER*
Blooms throughout the
summer

SCARLET RUNNER BEAN*
Phaseolus coccineus
Grows to 10 feet
Annual
The plant will "run" along the ground unless some form of trellis is provided
Well-drained, well-composted soil
Full sun

BEGONIA†
The flowering season is now at its height.

PETUNIA†
The flowers continue until late in summer

ROSEMARY†
Flowers are pretty well absent for the summer

ABUTILON
(Flowering maple)
Abutilon hybridum
Grows to 10 feet
Evergreen
Needs extra protection for winter north of Zone 8
Well-drained, loamy soil
Full sun

JAPANESE HONEYSUCKLE†
Flowers will remain on the plant at least through mid-summer

Begonia

FUCHSIA
Fuchsia spp.
Grows to 5 feet
Deciduous
Fairly pest-free
Moist, but well-drained, and fertile soil
Full sun

ORANGE TREE
Citrus sinensis
Grows to 30 feet
Evergreen in southern zones
Many varieties are not well-adapted for life north of Zone 8
Well-composted soil
Full sun

---

*For gardening facts, see pages 50-1.

†For gardening facts, see pages 26-7.

SHELTER, SHADE, AND SUNLIGHT

When we think of humming-birds, one of the first visions to come to mind is one of constant motion. A majority of us have never seen a hummingbird that was not in motion. However, the tiny motion-factories do in fact spend all but about 20-25 percent of their time perched and not in flight. Our misconception is fostered by the birds' tendency to leave their perches for feeding every quarter-hour or so throughout the day.

A hummingbird's favourite perch will be within a short flight to a ready supply of nectar and tiny insects. Mature males will make do with nearly any handy branch, regardless of the amount of shelter it offers. Females and immature birds are more comfortable with some cover over and around their perches. Nests will almost always be built in sheltered locations.

At the same time, humming-birds generally favor feeding areas with plenty of open, sunny, non-sheltered space around the plants where they take their nectar. Such open areas, luckily, also provide better viewing of the birds as they cavort around the flower beds.

In general, an area designed to attract hummingbirds should be no more than one-third shaded, either fully or partially. The shaded area should be no more than 20-30 feet from the open areas and flower beds, although the shade should not fall across either of these other areas.

▶ *Hummingbirds prefer gardens that provide perching locations in close proximity to the flowers where they take nectar.*

THE HUMMINGBIRD BATH

We don't often think of hummingbirds needing water, and in fact they do get much of the liquid they need each day – about seven times their body weight – from the nectar on which they feed. However they will take advantage of any fresh-water sources that they find.

Traditional birdbaths and in-ground mini-ponds don't offer much for hummingbirds, unless they have been specially adapted. Most songbirds in our backyards require very shallow water for bathing –

no more than an inch or two – but hummingbirds need areas that are even more shallow than that. Generally a quarter- to a half-inch is their maximum depth. The tiny birds often bathe and drink from such small water sources as dew collection in the curve of a plant's leaf.

Most structures we use to provide water for birds are deeper than this and will need to be modified with extra layers of pebbles, large-grain sand and the like to accommodate bathing hummingbirds.

On the other hand, humming-birds will use traditional birdbaths for drinking and limited bathing. They'll zip across the water there, just touching the surface with their breast feathers and wing tips, and dipping their bills down for a sip or two.

In addition, hummingbirds have shown a decided preference for water in the form of mist or gentle spray, through which they can fly repeatedly. Lawn sprinklers and miniature waterfalls in mini-ponds provide this type of water and are visited regularly.

◀▶ *While hummingbirds get most of the water they need as part of the nectar they draw from flowers, they will not pass up the opportunity for some drinking and bathing. Traditional birdbaths will serve them just fine. However, misting, sprinkling and other moving water, like this fountain, has an added appeal.*

INSECTS, TOO, FOR FOOD

We tend to see hummingbirds and nectar as completely complementary to one another. We tend to think that nectar, and the artificial nectar that we offer, provides the full diet of the hummingbirds in our gardens. Many early attempts to maintain the birds in captivity failed because of this belief.

However, the simple fact is that a hummingbird cannot survive on a diet of nectar alone. Insects are an important part of the diet as well.

Ants, small beetles, tiny flies, wasps, spiders and similar creatures are all included in the hummingbird diet. The tiny birds are regularly observed diving like miniature hawks through swarms of insects. They often hover at a spider web to pluck out some recently snared insect. And, those repeated visits to favored flowers provide not only nectar, but the insects that the nectar has attracted as well.

Hummingbirds consume an incredibly large number of insects. They must because their metabolism runs so high. Depending upon the species, a hummingbird can burn more than 12,000 calories per day. Tests have shown that an entire stomachful of insects can be completely digested in less than 15 minutes.

▶ *Hummingbirds eat a great many more insects than most casual observers realize. They take most of their insects alive and on the wing, but they will also take advantage of spider web victims.*

2,500   12,000
calories per day

THE EARLY FALL GARDEN

As fall begins to take hold of the garden and many of the flowering plants begin to lose their blooms, most of the local hummingbird population – across most of North America – will begin to disappear. Their annual southward migration is underway.

Although nearly all hummingbirds – except a confused straggler or so – will be gone from much of the continent by mid- to late fall, in most gardens the exodus actually begins earlier than it really must. This is because most gardens are not planted to provide continuing blooms into the fall. In addition, many gardeners take down their hummingbird feeders as soon as the birds' numbers seem to be declining.

The answer to the second part of this equation is the easier to counteract: maintain feeders further into the fall.

For the problem of declining blooms late in the season, we might consider some plants with longer blooming seasons. Some of these that also have strong attraction for hummingbirds include balsam, cardinal flower, hollyhock, larkspur, the various monkey-flower species, nasturtium, the various paintbrush species, petunia, phlox, salvia, spiderflower and zinnia.

Some trees and shrubs also can be employed to provide "off-season" blooms. These include honeysuckle, eucalyptus, flowering gum, orange, swamp mahogany and tree tobacco.

◀ *Long-flowering cultivars, such as these petunias, will hold their flowers well into the fall, continuing to attract hummers.*

EARLY FALL GARDEN

1 *Red-hot poker*
2 *Fuchsia*
3 *Lemon bottlebrush*
4 Ocotillo
5 *Shrimp plant*
6 *Lantana*
7 *Monkey flower*
8 *Nicotiana*
9 *Abutilon*
10 *Scarlet runner bean*
11 *Trumpet vine*

EARLY FALL PLANTS

Nicotiana

RED-HOT POKER
Kniphofia (Tritoma) uvaria
Grows to 4 feet
Perennial
From Zone 7 north this plant needs a winter mulch
Well-drained soil
Sun-loving

FUCHSIA*
Except in the southern zones, the flowers are now disappearing from the plant

---

*For gardening facts, see pages 38-9.

LEMON BOTTLEBRUSH
Callistemon citrinus
Grows to 10 feet
Evergreen
Requires extra winter protection north of Zone 8
Well-composted, sandy soil
Full sun

OCOTILLO
Fouquieria splendens
Grows to 25 feet
Deciduous
Needs extra protection in winter north of Zone 8
Well-drained soil
Full sun

SHRIMP PLANT†
Except in the southern
zones, the flowers are
now disappearing

LANTANA†
The flowers are beginning
to disappear

MONKEY FLOWER
Mimulus cardinalis
Grows to 1 foot
Perennial
Will self-seed and expand
bed area on its own
Well-composted, moist
soil
Partial shade

NICOTIANA*
The flowers will
disappear by mid-fall in
nearly all regions

ABUTILON*
Except in the southern
zones, the flowers are
now gone

SCARLET
RUNNER BEAN*
The flowering season is
past for this plant

TRUMPET VINE
Campsis radicans
Grows to 30 feet
Deciduous vine
One of the very best
hummingbird plants
Well-drained, well-
composted soil
Full sun

---

†For gardening facts, see
pages 26-7.

Fuchsia

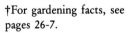

A WILDFLOWER OPTION

Interest in wildflowers as garden and backyard plants has been growing apace in recent years across the country. There's a certain mystique about planting and growing these species, a special feeling of connectedness to what was frontier and wild America.

This is a very helpful trend from the viewpoint of hummingbirds. Wild species generally offer more blooms and more nectar at each bloom than the domestic species that man has cultivated from them. In addition, hummingbirds evolved with those wildflower species and those are the blooms they learned to thrive upon long before humans even dreamt of cultivation.

It is similarly good news for many gardeners. Often the wildflower species are easier to establish in the garden, able to thrive on a wider range of environmental types, and requiring less care and attention than their domesticated counterparts.

In the eastern half of the continent, cardinal flower, wild columbine, jewelweed and salvia are very good starting points for wildflowers in the garden. Various paintbrush and monkeyflower species are widely employed across the West. In the dry regions of the American Southwest, century plants and ocotillos have brought favorable results.

▶ *The wildflower garden or meadow is an increasingly attractive option for many gardeners. Employing plants native to a region proves equally attractive to hummingbirds.*

WILDFLOWER OPTION

1 *Butterfly bush*
2 *Scarlet sage*
3 *Wild columbine*
4 *Lupine*
5 *Coral bells*
6 *Lousewort*
7 *Jewelweed*
8 *Indian paintbrush*
9 *Bee balm*
10 *Cardinal flower*
11 *Trumpet honeysuckle*

WILDFLOWERS

BUTTERFLY BUSH
Buddleia davidii
Grows to 10 feet
Deciduous
An important
hummingbird plant
Slightly alkaline soil
Full sun

Butterfly bush

SCARLET SAGE
Salvia splendens
Grows to 2 feet
Perennial
A very long-lasting
flowering season
Well-composted soil
Sun or shade

WILD COLUMBINE
Aquilegia canadensis
Grows to 2 feet
Perennial
The rootstocks tend to
be deep-seated
Adaptable to a wide
range of soil conditions
Full or partial sun

LUPINE
Lupinus spp.
Grows to 3 feet
Perennial or annual
Needs to be restarted
each year in northern
zones
Adaptable to a wide
range of soil conditions
Full sun

CORAL BELLS
Heuchera sanguinea
Grows to 2 feet
Perennial
A dainty appearance
belies the resilience of
this plant
Adaptable to a wide
range of soil conditions
Full or partial sun

LOUSEWORT
Pedicularis canadensis
Grows to 2 feet
Perennial
Spreads very quickly
Adaptable to a wide
range of soil conditions
Full sun

JEWELWEED
Impatiens capensis
Grows to 2 feet
Annual
Must be restarted
each year
Moist, acidic soil
Partial sun

INDIAN PAINTBRUSH
Castilleja coccinea
Grows to 1½ feet
Perennial
Spreads quickly
Well-composted soil
Full sun

BEE BALM
Monarda didyma
Grows to 3 feet
Perennial
Ranks among the best
hummingbird plants
Adaptable to a wide
range of soil conditions
Full sun

CARDINAL FLOWER
Lobelia cardinalis
Grows to 3 feet
Perennial
Plants started from seed
generally will not flower
until second season
Moist soil
Partial sun

TRUMPET HONEYSUCKLE
Lonicera sempervirens
Grows to 10 feet
Semi-evergreen
Can take over a
garden area
Well-drained soil
Partial sun

Jewelweed

SPECIAL RELATIONSHIPS

For many gardeners the glimpse of a hummingbird flitting about their flowers is cause for surprise. To them the birds, largely because of their small size and amazing speed, seem so wild and so evasive. They would never dream that individual relationships are possible with the tiny birds.

However, with just a bit of effort and patience, hummingbirds will grow accustomed to the presence of humans close to and directly in their feeding areas. Over time, they can become downright pesky in their demands for a refilling of their feeders.

The key is to be able to spend at least a little time in the garden every day throughout the period, spring through early fall, when the hummingbirds are present. Lawn furniture or a bench can allow you to sit and remain quite still during the early stages of familiarizing the birds with your presence, an absolutely necessary first step.

At first the hummingbirds will be apprehensive and aloof. They may even abandon their normal feeding areas temporarily. After just a few days, however, they will come to accept your presence. Soon they will be darting quite close on their regular trips for nectar and insects. It is not all that uncommon for a particularly patient person to have one or a few birds that will eventually perch on his or her finger. Concerns over "teaching" the birds to become too tame are warrantless. Hummingbirds will never lose their innate "flightiness" regardless of the amount of conditioning and time spent with them.

COMMON HUMMINGBIRDS

A directory of all the species of hummingbirds that inhabit North America is not nearly as lengthy as many newcomers to the passion at first believe. While a few species are very common over a widespread range, such as the ruby-throated hummingbird in the east and the black-chinned hummingbird in the west, most occupy much smaller ranges, within which they might be quite common. The limited number of species, the tight ranges of many, and the distinct markings of most makes for easier identification than with most other bird families.

◀ *The Ruby-throated Hummingbird is one of the most numerous and widespread of the North American species. It is also the only species to nest east of the Mississippi River.*

♂

ALLEN'S HUMMINGBIRD
Selasphorous sasin

Range: Breeding, Pacific Coast, south
from southern Oregon; Wintering,
southern Arizona and Gulf Coast
of Texas
Habitat: Wooded areas

ANNA'S HUMMINGBIRD
Calypte anna

Range: Breeding and wintering, Pacific
Coast south from southern Canada and
east in southern Arizona
Habitat: Wooded and chaparral areas

♂

BERYLLINE HUMMINGBIRD
Amazilia beryllina

Range: Breeding, mostly south of the
U.S.-Mexican border but also into
southern Texas, New Mexico and
Arizona
Habitat: In and near wooded areas

<u>BLACK-CHINNED</u> <u>HUMMINGBIRD</u>
Archilochus alexandri

Range: Breeding, southwestern and
western U.S. north into southern British
Columbia
Habitat: Very widespread

<u>BLUE-THROATED</u> <u>HUMMINGBIRD</u>
Lampornis clemenciae

Range: Breeding, southern Arizona and
southwestern Texas
Habitat: Wooded areas, usually near
streams

♂

♀

<u>BROAD-BILLED</u> <u>HUMMINGBIRD</u>
Selasphorus platycercus

Range: Breeding, California east to
Great Basin, Wyoming south into
Mexico
Habitat: Widespread, but generally near
wooded areas

♂

BROAD-TAILED
HUMMINGBIRD
Selasphorus platycercus

Range: Breeding, southern Idaho and
Wyoming south to the U.S.-Mexican
border
Habitat: Higher elevations

♂

BUFF-BELLIED HUMMINGBIRD
Amazilia yucatanensis

Range: Gulf Coast of Texas
Habitat: Along streams

<u>CALLIOPE HUMMINGBIRD</u>
Stellula calliope

Range: Breeding, western Canada
and U.S.
Habitat: Mountainous regions

COSTA'S HUMMINGBIRD
Calypte costae

Range: Breeding, southwestern U.S.;
Wintering, slightly north of the
U.S.-Mexican border
Habitat: Wide-ranging from urban areas
to desert regions

<u>LUCIFER HUMMINGBIRD</u>
Calothorax lucifer

Range: Breeding, mostly south of the
U.S.-Mexican border, but also into
southwestern Texas and southeastern
Arizona
Habitat: Open arid and desert locations

MAGNIFICENT HUMMINGBIRD
Eugense fulgens

Range: Breeding, southern Colorado
south to the U.S.-Mexican border
Habitat: Mountain and hill regions

♂

<u>RUBY-THROATED</u>
<u>HUMMINGBIRD</u>
Archilochus colubris

Range: Breeding, eastern half of the
continent
Habitat: Generally near, but not
exclusively in, wooded areas

RUFOUS HUMMINGBIRD
Selasphorus rufus

Range: Breeding, southwestern Canada
and northwestern U.S., south into
northern California and Montana
Habitat: Wooded areas, often
coniferous

VIOLET-CROWNED HUMMINGBIRD
Amazilia verticalis

Range: Breeding, southeastern Arizona
and occasionally southeastern California
Habitat: In canyons and along streams

<u>WHITE-EARED</u> <u>HUMMINGBIRD</u>
Hylocharis leucotis

Range: Breeding, southeastern Arizona
Habitat: Wooded mountain areas

COLLECTIONS TO VISIT

Some of the American zoos that
include hummingbirds in their
collections, generally in special
aviaries, are:

Arizona Sonora Desert Museum,
2021 N. Kinney Road, Tucson,
AZ 85743.

Brookfield Zoo,
Brookfield, IL 60513.

Columbus Zoo,
P.O. Box 400, Powell, OH 43065.

**Cincinnati Zoo and Botanical
Gardens,**
3400 Vine St., Cincinnati, OH 45220.

Denver Zoo,
2300 Steel St., Denver, CO 80205.

Indianapolis Zoo,
1200 W. Washington St., Indianapolis,
IN 46222.

Philadelphia Zoo,
3400 W. Girard Ave., Philadelphia,
PA 19104.

San Diego Zoo,
P.O. Box 551, San Diego, CA 92112.

▲ *The hummingbird garden need not exclude human use. Paths and* *bridges can be fully incorporated with delightful results.*

INDEX

ACKNOWLEDGMENTS

All images in this book are the
copyright of Quarto Publishing
Inc. except for the following:
Diane Calkins *9;* Gregory K.
Scott *18, 19;* Photo/Nats *12, 29;*
Unicorn Stock Photos *7, 8, 17,
20, 21, 23, 31, 33, 34*-*5, 41, 43,
46*-*7, 53, 59, 77.*

Index by Hazel Bell